The Greatest of These

The Greatest of These

*Quotations on
Fundamental Truths of Charity—
The Teachings of Freemasonry*

Woodrow W. Morris

Macoy Publishing & Masonic Supply Co., Inc.
Richmond, Virginia

Printed in the United States of America

Dedicated to my wife

INABELLE

Who knows the full meaning of "The Greatest of These..."

FOREWORD

Ever since that ancient moment when man first asked the fateful question: "Am I my brother's keeper?," the answer has come echoing and reverberating across the centuries and throughout the universe: "Yes! You are your brother's keeper!"

This volume provides brief glimpses of some of the many and varied expressions of thoughtful people of all ages as they have paid testimony to that love and charity which serve to set us apart from the beasts of the field. These are fundamental truths. They form the bases of organized religions; they are embodied in the considerations of poets and philosophers; they are the central core of the teachings, precepts and ideals of Freemasonry; they are building blocks of governments; and they are a part of the daily lives and considerations of mankind in general. Thus this compilation of poetry, verse, proverb, and prose focuses attention on the wisdom of the ages as writers of all times reflect their deep convictions concerning man's necessary humanity toward man.

The entries in this book cover all the divisions noted above, thus providing the broadest possible coverage of the basic concepts of charity. It is hoped these quotations will lead the reader to search further for additional examples of the meaning of charity in the daily lives of all of us. By so doing perhaps we may be stimulated to exercise our concern for those among us who need our attention, and by so doing help to make this world a better place in which to live.

The 1983 Nobel Laureate in literature, William Golding, had this to say in his acceptance speech: "Either we blow ourselves off the face of the Earth or we degrade the fertility of the Earth bit by bit until we have ruined it." He then expressed his faith that we could prevent it. "Words may, through the devotion, the skill, the passion, and the luck of writers, prove to be the most powerful thing in the world.

"They may move men to speak to each other because some of these words somewhere express not just what the writer is thinking but what a huge segment of the world is thinking.

"They may allow man to speak to man, the man in the street to speak to his fellow until a ripple becomes a tide running through every nation — of common sense, of simple healthy caution, a tide that rulers and negotiators cannot ignore so that nation truly does speak to nation.

"Go back. Step back now. Agreement between you does not need cleverness, elaboration, maneuvers. It needs common sense and, above all, a daring generosity."

These examples of such daring generosity, of the breadth of meaning of charity may not alter immediately human behavior around the globe. On the other hand, perhaps the pleasant stimulation of these quotations will help make a start toward the kind of world revolution envisaged by Golding, by the original authors of these statements, and by all of us.

January, 1985   WOODROW W. MORRIS

PREFACE

Compassion or charity is one of the noblest attributes of man. This collection of thoughts, this distillation of reflections from many sources and untold generations, attempts to bring into our materialistic world some of the generosity and benevolence of those who have gone before us. These are fundamental precepts of Freemasonry.

I know of no one better qualified or more spiritually motivated to do this work than Dr. W. W. Morris, Past Grand Master. He has an inborn thread of compassion for his fellow man that runs throughout his life. This compassion extends to all, regardless of their feelings or attitudes toward him. He is the epitome of the Biblical lesson to "turn the other cheek."

His work at The University of Iowa as a Professor and Associate Dean of the College of Medicine, and his involvement in various governmental projects regarding the aging, along with his work in the charity programs for the Masons of Iowa, have qualified and endeared him to all who know him.

May those who read this labor of love have a better appreciation of the generosity of their fellow human beings, a better understanding of the meaning of charity, compassion, and love for one another.

C. GLENN BROWN
Grand Master of Masons in Iowa
1983-1984

EDITOR'S NOTE

In compiling these materials many sources were examined in which quotations were searched out based on the following KEY WORDS deemed synonymous with or closely related to the meaning of charity:

alms	compassion	kind-heartedness	philanthropy
almsgiving	generosity	kindliness	sympathy
altruism	gift	kindness	tenderness
beneficence	giving	liberality	unselfishness
benevolence	goodness	love	
benignity	helpfulness	magnanimity	
bounty	humanity	munificence	

Readers finding or knowing of additional quotations may send them to: Woodrow W. Morris, c/o Macoy Publishing Co., 3011 Dumbarton Road, Richmond, VA 23228-0759, for possible inclusion in revisions of this compilation.

ACKNOWLEDGEMENTS

Appreciation is expressed to the publishers, authors, agents, and copyright owners who have granted permission to reprint from the works listed below. The listing is alphabetical by authors or by the person or agency granting permission.

Jean Bernard-Luc and Jean Anouilh, scenarists for the motion picture *Monsieur Vincent* and NBC Enterprise, a Division of the National Broadcasting Company; Pearl Buck, "The Quest" from *Words of Love,* Harper & Row Publishers, Inc.; Martin Buxbaum, "Brotherhood" and two other poems from *The Warm World of Martin Buxbaum,* Acropolis Books Ltd.; Carl Claudy, a statement on Masonic Charity, The Masonic Service Association of the United States; Henry Clausen 33°, Sovereign Grand Commander, The Supreme Council 33°, A.A.S.R., selections from *Morals and Dogma* and from *The New Age;* Henry Doster, "Masonic Charity," The New Age, February, 1983; Tom Eggleston, Grand Secretary, Grand Lodge of Iowa A.F. & A.M., material from *History of the Grand Lodge of Iowa, A.F. & A.M.,* Kahlil Gibran, "On Giving," from *The Prophet*, Alfred A. Knopf, Inc.; E. H. Gulick, a song composed for the Abu Bekr Shrine Chanters, Sioux City, Iowa; Donald E. Krueger, Editor, *The Bulletin of the Masonic Relief Association;* Chester R. MacPhee, "Masons: Knights of Charity," *The New Age,* November, 1981; Charles Menge, "Reach Out and Touch Someone" in *The Short Talk Bulletin of The Masonic Service Association,* Vol. 60, No. 7; John D. Rockefeller, Jr., "I Believe," The Rockefeller Foundation; Franklin Delano

Roosevelt, *The Public Papers and Addresses of Franklin Delano Roosevelt,* Random House, Inc.; Carl Sandburg, portions of *Remembrance Rock,* Harcourt Brace Jovanovich, Inc.; Albert Schweitzer, portions of *The Philosophy of Civilization,* Monsieur Gustave Woytt representing the literary rights of the Albert Schweitzer Estate; Dwight L. Smith, *Whither Are We Traveling?,* *The Indiana Freemason.*

Deep appreciation is also expressed for the creative art work of Ann Layman Chancellor, formerly of the University of Iowa and now at New Orleans University.

Vignettes by James Ford.

CONTENTS

ACCORDING TO PROPHETS & APOSTLES

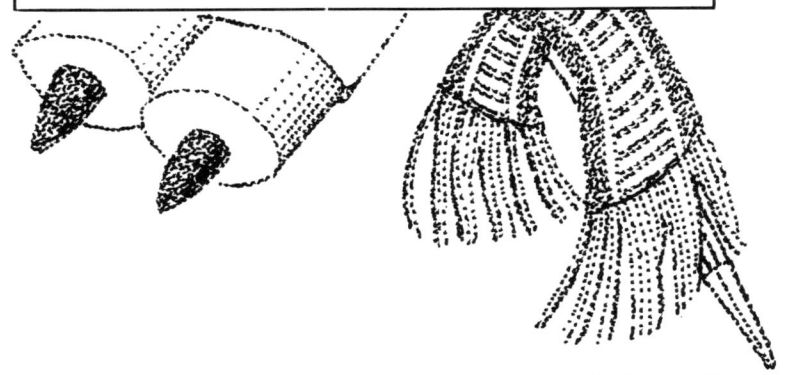

Ann Layman Chancellor

If your enemy is hungry, give
him bread to eat;
and if he is thirsty, give him
water to drink;

— The Holy Bible
Proverbs 25: 21

The stranger who sojourns with you
shall be to you as a native among you,
and you shall love him as yourself . . .

— The Holy Bible
Leviticus 19: 34

When you reap your harvest in your field,
and have forgotten a sheaf in the field,
you shall not go back to get it;
it shall be for the soujourner, the fatherless,
and the widow;
that the Lord your God may bless you
in all the work of your hands.
When you beat your olive trees,
you shall not go over the boughs again;
it shall be for the sojourner, the fatherless,
and the widow.
When you gather the grapes of your vineyard,
you shall not glean it afterward;
it shall be for the sojourner, the fatherless,
and the widow.

— The Holy Bible
Deuteronomy 24: 19-21

Ann Layman Chancellor

And behold, a lawyer stood up to put him to the test, saying, "Teacher, what shall I do to inherit eternal life?" He said to him, "What is written in the law? How do you read?" And he answered, "You shall love the Lord your God with all your heart, and with all your soul, and with all your strength, and with all your mind; and your neighbor as yourself." And he said to him, "You have answered right; do this and you will live." But he, desiring to justify himself, said to Jesus, "And who is my neighbor?" Jesus replied, "A man was going down from Jerusalem to Jericho, and he fell among robbers, who stripped him and beat him, and departed leaving him half-dead. Now by chance a priest was going down that road; and when he saw him he passed by on the other side. So likewise a Levite, when he came to the place and saw him, passed by on the other side. But a Samaritan, as he journeyed, came to where he was; and when he saw him, he had compassion, and went to him and bound up his wounds, pouring on oil and wine; then he set him on his own beast and brought him to an inn, and took care of him. And the next day he took out two denarii and gave them to the innkeeper, saying, 'Take care of him; and whatever more you spend, I will repay you when I come back.' Which of these three, do you think, proved neighbor to the man who fell among the robbers?"

He said, "The one who showed mercy on him."

And Jesus said to him. "Go and do likewise."

— The Holy Bible
Luke 10: 25-37

5

Let your light so shine before men,
that they may see your good works,
and glorify your Father which is in
heaven.

— The Holy Bible
Matthew 5: 16

Then saith he also to them that bade him, When thou makest a
dinner or a supper, call not thy friends, nor thy brethren, neither
thy kinsmen, nor thy rich neighbors; lest they also bid thee again,
and a recompense be made. But when thou makest a feast, call
the poor, the maimed, the lame, the blind; and thou shalt be
blessed; for they cannot recompense thee: for thou shalt be
recompensed at the resurection of the just.

— The Holy Bible
Luke 14: 12-14

Though I speak with the tongues of men and of angels, and have not charity, I am become as sounding brass, or a tinkling cymbal. And though I have the gift of prophecy, and understand all mysteries, and all knowledge; and though I have faith, so that I could remove mountains, and have not charity, I am nothing. And though I bestow all my worldly goods to feed the poor, and though I give my body to be burned, and have not charity, it profiteth me nothing. Charity suffereth long, and is kind; charity envieth not; charity vaunteth not itself, is not puffed up, Doth not behave itself unseemly, seeketh not her own, is not easily provoked, thinketh no evil; Rejoiceth not in iniquity, but rejoiceth in the truth; Beareth all things, believeth all things, hopeth all things, endureth all things. Charity never faileth; but where there be prophecies, they shall fail; whether there be tongues, they shall cease; whether there be knowledge, it shall vanish away. But when that which is perfect is come, then that which is in part shall be done away. When I was a child, I spake as a child, I thought as a child; but when I became a man, I put away childish things. For now we see through a glass, darkly; but then face to face: now I know in part; but then I shall know even as I also am known. And now abideth faith, hope, and charity, these three; but the greatest of these is charity.

— *The Holy Bible*
I Corinthians 13

Benevolence, righteousness, propriety,
and knowledge are not infused into us
from without.

Benevolence is man's mind, and righteousness is man's path.
— *Meng-tzu (Mencius)*
The Chinese Classics, Vol. II
The Works of Mencius, Book VI
1:6.7 and 1:11.1

Benevolence is the distinguishing characteristic
of man. As embodied in man's conduct, it is called
the path of duty.

He who wishes to be benevolent will not be so rich.
— *Meng-tzu (Mencius)*
Discourses, VII

8

The world rests upon three things: doctrine,
the service of God, and benevolence.

— *Simon II, the Just*

The noblest charity is to prevent a man from
accepting charity and the best alms are to
enable man to dispense with alms.

Loving kindness is greater than laws; and the
charities of life are more than all ceremonies.

— *Talmud*

A Roman asked Rabbi Akiba: "If as you say, your god loves the
poor, why does he not support them?"

A reasonable question, certainly. Rabbi Akiba replied that if
God left the care of the poor to the benevolence of the Jews, it was
purposely "so that we may be saved by its merits from the punish-
ment of Gehinnom (Gehenna or Purgatory)." Akiba cited this
passage from the book of Isaiah (58:7) as his authority:

Is it not to deal thy bread to the hungry,

And that thou bring the poor that are cast out to thy house?

When thou seest the naked, that thou cover him,

And that thou hid thyself from thine own flesh?

— *The Talmud*

If the poor asks of you and you have nothing in your hand to give him, soothe him with words. It is forbidden to rebuke a poor man or to raise one's voice against him in a shout, for his heart is shattered and crushed and it is written, "A broken and contrite heart, O God, you will not despise." And it is written, "I dwell in the high and holy place and also with him who is of a contrite and humble spirit, to revive the spirit of the humble and to revive the heart of the contrite." Alas for anyone who has humiliated a poor man, alas for him. He should rather be like a father both with compassion and with words, as it is written, "I was a father to the poor . . ."

There are eight degrees in the giving of charity, each one higher than that which follows it:

1. The highest degree, exceeded by none, is giving a gift or a loan or taking one as a partner or finding him employment by which he can be self-sustaining...

2. Giving charity to the poor without knowing to whom one gives, the recipient not knowing the donor's identity, for this is a good deed of intrinsic value, done for its own sake. An example of this is the Hall of Secret Donations which was maintained in the Temple. The righteous would donate in secret and the poor would be supported from it in secret. Approximating this is giving to a charity fund. One should not give to a charity fund unless he knows the collector is trustworthy and wise and conducts himself properly, like Rabbi Hananiah ben Traydon.

3. Giving to one whose identity one knows, although the recipient does not know the donor's identity. An example of this would be the action of those great sages who would walk about in secret and cast coins at the doors of the poor. It is fitting to imitate such a custom and it is a high degree indeed, if the charity collectors (through whom one can give impersonally) do not conduct themselves properly.

4. Giving without knowing to whom one gives, although the recipient knows the donor's identity. An example of this would be the action of those great sages who would wrap up coins in a bundle and throw it over their shoulder. The poor would then come to take it without suffering any embarrassment.
5. Giving before being asked.
6. Giving only after being asked.
7. Giving inadequately, though graciously.
8. Giving grudgingly.

The great sages would give a coin for the poor before each prayer service and then pray, as it is written, "I shall behold Your face in righteousness." Giving food to one's older sons and daughters (though one is not obligated to do so) in order to teach the males Torah and to direct the females on the proper path, and giving food to one's father and mother is considered to be charity. And it is a great degree of charity, for relatives should have precedence . . .

One should always press himself and suffer rather than be dependent upon others; he should not cast himself upon the community as a responsibility. Thus the sages commanded: "Rather make your Sabbath like a week day than be dependent upon others." Even if a man was learned and respected and then became poor he should occupy himself with a trade, even a lowly trade, rather than be dependent upon others. It is better to strip the hide of dead animals than to say "I am a great sage, I am a Priest; support me." Among the great sages there were wood choppers, those who watered gardens and those who worked with iron and charcoal. They did not ask the community for money and they did not take it when it was offered to them.

— *Maimonides (Moses ben Maimon)*
Mishneh Torah,
Hilkhot Matanot Aniyim

Every good act is charity.

Your smiling in your brother's face, is charity;

an exhortation of your fellowman to virtuous deeds, is equal to alms-giving;

your putting a wanderer on the right road, is charity;

your assisting the blind, is charity;

your removing stones, and thorns, and other obstructions from the road, is charity;

your giving water to the thirsty, is charity.

A man's true wealth hereafter, is the good he does in this world to his fellow-man.

When he dies, people will say, "What property has he left behind?"

But the angels will ask, "What good deeds has he sent before him?"

— Mahomet

Prayer carries us half-way to God,
fasting brings us to the door of his palace,
and alms-giving procures us admission.

— Koran

who loves with purity considers not the gift of the lover,
the love of the giver.

He is truly great, that is great in charity.

— Thomas á Kempis

Lord,
> make me an instrument of Your peace.
> Where there is hatred, let me sow love;
> Where there is injury, pardon;
> Where there is doubt, faith;
> Where there is despair, hope;
> Where there is darkness, light; and
> Where there is sadness, joy.

O divine Master.
> grant that I may not so much
> Seek to be consoled as to console;
> To be understood as to understand;
> To be loved as to love;
> For it is in giving that we receive;
> It is in pardoning that we are pardoned; and
> It is in dying that we are born to eternal life.

— St. Francis of Assisi

Charity is, indeed a great thing, and a gift of God,
and when it is rightly ordered, likens us to God himself,
as far as that is possible; for it is charity that makes the man.

Charity is the scope of all God's commands.

— St. John Chrysostom

The heart of a giver makes the gift dear and precious.

— Martin Luther

Everyone should give to charity. Even a poor man who is supported by charity should donate a portion of what he receives . . . If a man builds a house of worship, it should be more beautiful than his own home; if he provides food for the hungry, it ought to be the best on his table; if he gives clothing to the naked, it should come from the finest of his clothes.

— Rabbi Moses Isserles
Shulhan Arukh

The world is like a revolving wheel: one who is rich today
    may be poor tomorrow.
Let a man therefore give charity before the wheel has
    turned.

— Rabbi Israel al-Nakawa
Menoreth Hammar (Lamp of Illumination)

Whoever closes his eyes to this duty (to *tsedakah*-charity) and hardens his heart to his needy brother is called a worthless man, . . . Man must know that his is not the master of what he has, but only the guardian, to carry out the will of God who entrusted these things to his keeping . . .

— Rabbi Jacob ben Asher
The Tur

- True charity is sagacious, and will find out hints for beneficence.
- He hath riches sufficient, who hath enough to be charitable.
- Be charitable before wealth makes thee covetous.
- For this I think charity, to love God for himself, and our
  neighbor for God.

— Sir Thomas Browne

- Charity is the perfection and ornament of religion.
  - Charity is a virtue of the heart and not of the hands.
    - Gifts and alms are the expression not the essence
      of this virtue.

—Joseph Addison

Get all you can without hurting your soul, your body, or
  your neighbor.
Save all you can, cutting off every needless expense.
Give all you can. Be glad to give, and ready to distribute;
  laying up in store for yourselves a good foundation
  against the time to come, that you may attain eternal
  life.

—John Wesley

Do all the good you can,
By all the means you can,
In all the ways you can,
In all the places you can,
At all the times you can,
To all the people you can,
As long as ever you can.

—John Wesley

Ann Layman Chancellor

You will soon learn that charity is a
heavy burden to carry, heavier than the
kettle of soup and the basket of bread,
but you must keep your gentleness and
your smile. It's not enough to give
soup and bread—that the rich can do.
You are the little servant of the poor,
the Maid of Charity, always smiling and
in good humor. They are your masters,
terribly sensitive and exacting, as you
will see. But the uglier and dirtier
they are, the more unjust and bitter,
the more you must give them of your love.
It is only because of your love, *only*
your love, that the poor will forgive
you the bread you give them.

— *Monsieur Vincent*

God has so ordered that men, being in need of each other, should learn to love each other, and bear each other's burdens.

— *George Augustus Sala*

As lightening springs out of its concealment in dark clouds to flash through the world, so the divine light imbedded in matter emerges through charitable deeds . . . Thus, through charity, a sort of divine revelation occurs in the soul.

— *Shneor Zalman of Lyady*

Charity is a magnet with more power to attract the divine influence than any other precept.

— *Shneor Zalman of Lyady*

We believe in being honest, true,
chaste, benevolent, virtuous, and
in doing good to all men; indeed,
we may say that we follow the
admonition of Paul—
We believe all things,
we hope all things,
we have endured many things, and
hope to endure all things.
If there is anything virtuous,
lovely, or of good report or praiseworthy,
we seek after these things.

— *Joseph Smith*

The soldier who dies to save his brother
reaches the highest degrees of charity,
and this is the virtue of a single act of charity:
it cancels a whole lifetime of sin.

— Cardinal Désiré Joseph Mercier

Be charitable in your thoughts, in your speech
    and in your actions.
Be charitable in your judgments, in your attitudes
    and in your prayers.
Think charitably of your friends, your neighbors,
    your relatives, and even your enemies.
And if there be those whom you can help in a material way,
    do so in a quiet, friendly, neighborly way,
    as if it were the most common and
    everyday experience for you.
Tongues of men and angels, gifts of prophecy and
    all mysteries and all knowledge are as nothing
    without charity.

— Cardinal Patrick Joseph Hayes

Proverbs from Divers Religions

Buddhism:
- Save thyself by giving; what is given is well saved.
- Liberality, courtesy, kindliness, and usefulness—these are to the world what the linchpin is to the rolling chariot.

Christianity and Judaism:
- Cast thy bread upon the waters; for thou shalt it after many days. (Ecclesiastes iii) find
- Thou shalt open thy hand unto thy brother, to thy poor, and to thy needy, in thy land. (Deuteronomy xv)
- Learn to do well; seek judgment, relieve the oppressed, plead for the widow. (Isaiah i)
- If thine enemy be hungry, give him bread to eat; if he be thirsty, give him water to drink. (Proverbs of Solomon xxv)
- Thou shalt love thy neighbor as thyself. (Matthew xix)

Confucianism:
- The tendency of man's nature to do good is like the tendency of water to flow downwards.

Hinduism:
- One satisfies the debt of his fellow-man by doing good to them.
- Help your brother's boat and your own will reach the shore.
- They who give have all things; they who withhold have nothing.

Islam: • Be constant in prayers and give alms.

Judaism: • Charity is the salt of riches.
                 • Take care of the children of the poor, for
                   from them will knowledge arise.
                 • If thou hast taken up God's trade, put on his
                   livery (i.e., charity), also.
                 • Loving-kindness is greater than laws; and
                   the charities of life are more than all ceremonies.
                 • Drain not the waters of thy well while others
                   may desire them.
                 • When an orphan asylum was in danger of clos-
                   ing because it lacked a certain sum of money,
                   the rabbi of the community urgently implored
                   the richest men in town to make up the deficit.
                   But the *nogid* (wealthy man) refused. "I will give
                   you my share in Paradise if only you will give
                   me the money," pleaded the rabbi out of
                   desperation. The rich man was delighted and
                   gave him the money. And so the orphans
                   asylum was saved, but the rabbi was without his
                   portion of bliss in the World-to-Come.
                   The rabbi's disciples were aghast when they
                   heard of this "deal." They remonstrated with
                   him: "Oh, Rabbi! How could you do such a
                   thing—you, a holy man, were sure to enter
                   Paradise." The rabbi replied: "Twice each day I
                   repeat my prayers: 'Love they God with all thy
                   heart, with all thy soul, and with all thy posses-
                   sions.' My sons, I'm only a poor man. With
                   what possessions can I serve God? All that I
                   possess is my share in Paradise, and to serve
                   God's children, the orphans, I am ready to part
                   even with that."

Sikh (India): • Without good works no one can be saved.

Sufism (Persia): • Generosity consists in doing justice and in not demanding justice.
• There are three signs of generosity — to keep faith without resistance, to praise without being incited thereto by liberality, and to give without being asked.

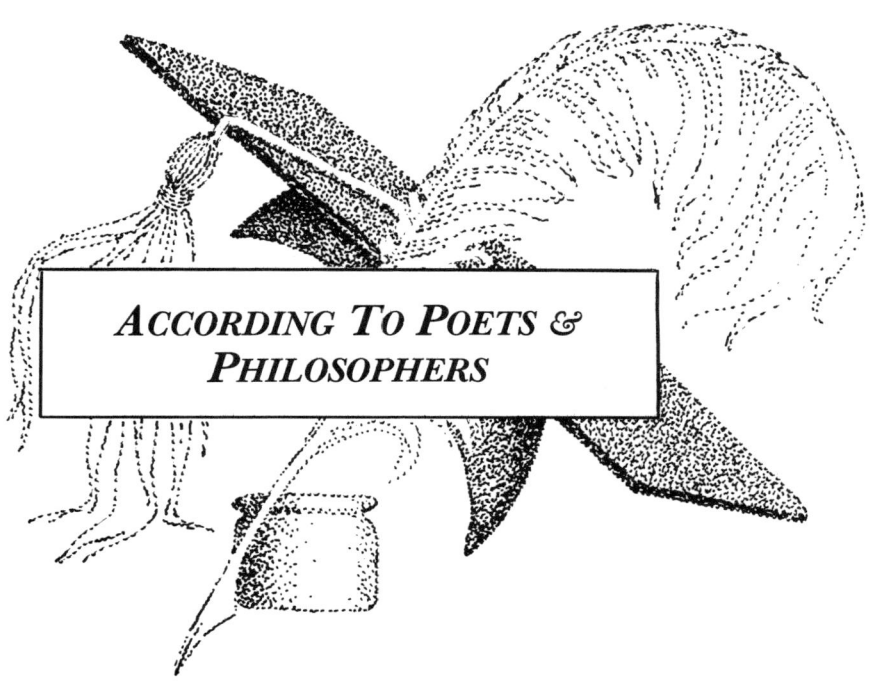

ACCORDING TO POETS & PHILOSOPHERS

Ann Layman Chancellor

Philanthropy, like charity, must begin at home; from this centre our sympathies should extend in an ever widening circle.

— *Charles Lamb*

Charity begins at home.
— *Publius Terentius Afer*
Andria (The Lady of Andros)

Liberty, like charity must begin at home.
— *James Bryant Conant*
Our Unique Heritage

Charity should begin at home but should not end there.
— *Scottish Proverb*

Let them learn first to show piety at home.
— *The Holy Bible*
I Timothy 5:4

But how shall we expect charity
    towards others,
When we are uncharitable to ourselves?
Charity begins at home, is the voice
    of the world;
Yet is every man his greatest enemy, and,
As it were, his own executioner.

— *Sir Thomas Browne*
Religio Medici

25

James Oglethorpe planned the colony of Georgia as an asylum for poor, imprisoned British debtors, for persecuted Protestants, for Jews, but not for Papists. A corporation was formed to govern the colony under a twenty-one year charter. The common seal of the corporation having on one side a group of silkworms at their toils, with the motto, *Non sibi, sed aliis* — "Not for themselves, but for others." — expressed the purpose of the patrons.

George Bancroft
History of the United States, Vol. 2

Virgil, when Bathyllus, a rival, had wrongly claimed a couplet in honour of Augustus, which had been found written on the palace door, wrote on the same door *"Hos ergo versicles feci, tulit alter honores"* ("I wrote these versicles, another carried off the credit of them.") Virgil then wrote four incomplete lines beginning *"Sic vos non vobis,"* and asked Bathyllus to complete them. He failed to do so. Then Virgil came forward, supplied the remainder of each line and vindicated his claim to the first couplet as well.

Sic vos non vobis, mellificatis, apes.
Sic vos non vobis, nidificatis, aves.
Sic vos non vobis, vellera fertis, oves.
Sic vos non vobis, fertis aratra, boves.

> Thus do you bees make honey, but not only for yourselves.
> Thus do you birds make nests, but not only for yourselves.
> Thus do you sheep make fleeces, but not only for yourselves.
> Thus do you oxen pull plows, but not only for yourselves.

— Virgil

It is heaven upon earth to have a man's mind move in charity, rest in providence, and turn upon the poles of truth.

— *Sir Francis Bacon*

The desire of power in excess caused the angels to fall;
the desire of knowledge in excess, caused man to fall;
but in charity there is no excess,
neither can angel or man come in danger by it.

— *Sir Francis Bacon*
Essays: Of Goodness

He that defers charity until he is dead is,
if a man weighs it rightly, rather liberal
of another man's rather than his own.

— *Sir Francis Bacon*
Collections of Sentences, no. 55

- Man resembles the gods in nothing so much as in doing good to their fellow creatures.
- In nothing do men approach so nearly to the gods as in doing good to men.

— *Cicero*

I would have a man generous to his country, his neighbor, his kindred, his friends, and most of all his poor friends. Not like some who are most lavish with those who are able to give the most to them.

— *Pliny, The Elder*

Charity is a naked child
giving honey to a bee
without wings.
— *Francis Quarles*
Enchiridion, II

The manner of giving is worth more than the gift.
— *Pierre Corneille*
Le Menteur, act I, scene I

Charity itself fulfills the law,
and who can sever love from charity.
— *William Shakespeare*
Love's Labour's Lost

Give, if thou canst, an alms;
if not, afford, instead of that,
a sweet and gentle word.
— *Robert Herrick*

Ambition, malice, rage and hate
Are strangers to my soul;
But peace and joy possess the parts,
And charity the whole.
— *Daniel Defoe*

All good things of this world are no further good than as they are
of use; and whatever we may reap up to give to others, we enjoy
only as much as we can make useful to ourselves and others, and
no more.

— *Daniel Defoe*

A decent provision for the poor is the true test of civilization.

> — *Samuel Johnson*
> From Boswell, *Life of Johnson*

Anticipate charity by preventing poverty; assist the reduced fellowman, either by a considerable gift, or a sum of money, or by teaching him a trade, or by putting him in the way of business, so that he may earn an honest livelihood, and not be forced to the dreadful alternative of holding out his hand for charity. This is the highest step and summit of charity's golden ladder.

> — *Moses ben Maimon (Maimonides)*
> *Charity's Eight Degrees*

To give aid to every poor man is far beyond the reach and power of every man . . . Care of the poor is incumbent on society as a whole.

> — *Benedict Spinoza*
> *Ethics*

Thus is the problem of Rich and Poor to be solved. The law of accumulation will be left free; the laws of distribution free. Individualism will continue, but the millionaire will be but a trustee of the poor; entrusted for a season with a great part of the increased wealth of the community, but administering it for the community far better than it could or would have done for itself.

> — *Andrew Carnegie*
> *Wealth*

To complain that life has no joys while there is a single creature whom we can relieve by our bounty, assist by our counsels, or enliven by our presence, is to lament the loss of that which we possess, and is just as rational as to die of thirst with the cup in our hands.

— William Melmoth, ("Sir Thomas Fitzosborne")

False happiness renders men stern and proud, and that happiness is never communicated. True happiness renders them kind and sensible, and that happiness is always shared.

— Charles Montesquieu

Nine requisites for contented living:
> Health enough to make work a pleasure.
> Wealth enough to support your needs.
> Strength enough to battle with difficulties and overcome them.
> Grace enough to confess your sins and forsake them.
> Patience enough to toil until some good deed is accomplished.
> Charity enough to see some good in your neighbor.
> Love enough to move you to be useful and helpful to others.
> Faith enough to make real the things of God.
> Hope enough to remove all anxious fears concerning the future.

—Johann Wolfgang von Goethe

That charity is bad which takes from independence its proper pride, and from mendicity its proper shame.

— Robert Southey

There are three lessons I would write,
   Three words, as with a burning pen,
In tracings of eternal light,
   Upon the hearts of men.

Have hope. Though clouds environ round
   And gladness hides her face in scorn,
Put off the shadows from thy brow;
   No night but hath its morn.

Have faith. Where'er thy bark is driven—
   The calm's disport, the tempest's mirth—
Know this: God rules the hosts of heaven,
   The inhabitants of earth.

Have love. Not love alone for one,
   But man, as man, thy brother call;
And scatter, like a circling sun,
   Thy charities on all.

— Friederich von Schiller
Three Words of Strength

On that best portion of a good man's life, his little, nameless, unremembered acts of kindness and of love.

— William Wordsworth

As frozen as charity.
— *Robert Southey*
The Soldier's Wife

Alas for the rarity
of Christian charity
Under the sun!
— *Thomas Hood*
The Bridge of Sighs

The organized charity
scrimped and iced,
In the name of a cautious,
statistical Christ.
—*John Boyle O'Reilly*
In Bohemia

O chime of sweet Saint Charity,
Peal soon that Easter morn
When Christ for all shall risen be,
And in all hearts new-born!
— *James Russell Lowell*

Oh, brother man, fold to thy heart thy brother;
where pity dwells, the peace of God is there.
— *John Greenleaf Whittier*

There never was a person who did
anything worth doing who did not
receive more than he gave.
— *Henry Ward Beecher*

There is a duty to the living more important
than any charity to the dead.
— *Edgar Allen Poe*

Careless their merits or their faults to scan,
His pity gave ere charity began.
Thus to relieve the wretched was his pride,
And e'en his failings lean'd to Virtue's side.

                 — *Oliver Goldsmith*

Whatever mitigates the woes, or increases the happiness of others,
is a just criterior of goodness.

                 — *Oliver Goldsmith*

The living need charity more than the dead.

                 — *George Arnold*

A poor man served by thee shall make thee rich.

                 — *Elizabeth Barrett Browning*

Guard within yourself that treasure kindness. Know how to give
without hesitation, how to lose without regret, how to acquire
without meanness.

                 — *George Sand*

When I give I give myself.
— Walt Whitman
Song of Myself

The only gift is a portion of myself.
— Ralph Waldo Emerson
Gifts

Not what we give, but what we share—
For the gift without the giver is bare;
Who gives himself with his alms feeds three—
Himself, his hungry neighbor, and me.
—James Russell Lowell
The Vision of Sir Launfal

I am only one,
But still I am one,
I cannot do everything,
But still I can do something;
And because I cannot do everything
I will not refuse to do the something
        that I can do.
— Edward Everett Hale
For the Lend-a-Hand Society

To look up and not down,
To look forward and not back,
To look out and not in—and
To lend a hand.
— Edward Everett Hale
Ten Times One is Ten

35

Ann Layman Chancellor

Abou Ben Adhem (may his tribe increase!)
Awoke one night from a deep dream of peace,
And saw within the moonlight in his room,
Making it rich like a lily in bloom,
An angel writing in a book of gold:
Exceeding peace had made Ben Adhem bold,
And to the presence in the room he said,
"What writest thou?" The vision raised its head,
And with a look made of all sweet accord,
Answered, "The names of those who love the Lord."
"And is mine one?" said Abou. "Nay, not so,"
Replied the angel. Abou spoke more low,
But cheerily still; and said, "I pray thee, then,
Write me as one that loves his fellow-man."

The angel wrote and vanished. The next night
It came again, with a great wakening light,
And showed the names who love of God had blessed, —
And, lo! Ben Adhem's name led all the rest!

— *James Henry Leigh Hunt*
Abou Ben Adhem

One can know nothing of giving aught
that is worthy to give unless
one also knows how to take.
> — *Havelock Ellis*
> *Little Essays of Love and Virtue*

I wonder why it is that we are not
all kinder to each other than we are.
How much the world needs it!
How easily it is done!
> — *Henry Drummond*

The kinds of gratitude:
The sudden kind we feel when we take;
the larger kind we feel when we give.
> — *Edwin Arlington Robinson*

Love is a questing spirit,
Seeking where to find
A human frame to live in,
A human heart to bind.
> — *Pearl Buck*
> *Words of Love*
> *The Quest*

The sole meaning of life is to serve humanity.
> — *Leo (Lyev) Tolstoi*

OPEN YOUR EYES

Open your eyes and look for some man, or some work for the sake of men, which needs a little time, a little friendship, a little sympathy, a little sociability, a little human toil. Perhaps it is a lonely person, or an embittered person, or an invalid, or some unfortunate inefficient, to whom you can be something. It may be an old man or it may be a child . . . Who can reckon up all the ways in which the priceless fund of impulse, man, is capable of exploitation! He is needed in every nook and corner. Therefore search and see if there is not someplace where you may invest your humanity . . . But do not be satisfied without some side line in which you give yourself as a man to men.

—*Albert Schweitzer*
The Philosophy of Civilization

Then said a rich man, Speak to us of Giving.

And he answered:

You give but little when you give of your possessions.

It is when you give of yourself that you truly give.

*   *   *

There are those who give little of the much which they have — and they give it for recognition and their hidden desire makes the gifts unwholesome.

And there are those who have little and give it all.

These are the believers in life and the bounty of life, and their coffer is never empty.

There are those who give with joy, and that joy is their reward.

And there are those who give with pain, and that pain is their baptism.

And there are those who give and know not pain in giving, nor do they seek joy, nor give with mindfulness of virtue;

They give as in yonder valley the myrtle breathes its fragrance into space.

Through the hands of such as these God speaks, and from behind their eyes He smiles upon the earth.

It is well to give when asked, but it is better to give unasked, through understanding;

And to the open-handed the search for one who shall receive is joy greater than giving.

And is there aught you would withhold?

All you have shall some day be given;

Therefore give now, that the season of giving may be yours and not your inheritors'.

You often say, "I would give, but only to the deserving."

The trees in the orchards say not so, nor the flocks in your pasture.

They give that they may live, for to withhold is to perish.

*   *   *

— *Kahlil Gibran*
The Prophet

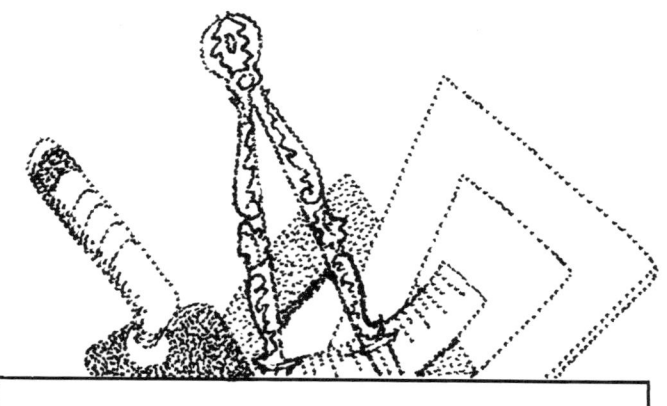

ACCORDING TO FREEMASONS

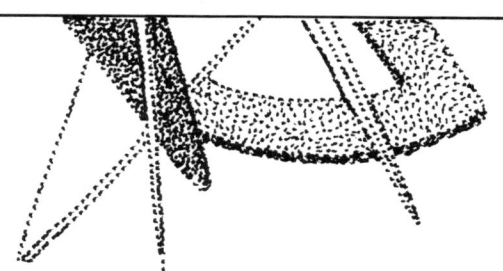

Ann Layman Chancellor

We, under subscribers, do hereby protest by all the oaths we received at our entry to the benefit of the Mason Word, that we shall own and maintain the Mason Box of Aberdeen, and of this our Lodge according as we have begun as the authors of it, and shall employ any money therein, or shall be put therein, to no other end but for the use and maintenance of our distressed Brethren, especially those of our own Lodge . . .

As for their children belonging to our Lodge if their parents have lived honestly and virtuously . . . and if these children be virtuously inclined . . . we are obliged to see them educated and put to schools and trades according to their inclinations . . .

Therefore, let all of you, who are, or shall be, our successors in the Mason Craft, follow our example, and let not your poor have occasion to curse you, and in the due performance of the above (you) will occasion the blessing of God to accompany all your endeavors, which is the hearty wish of us all who are the authors hereof. Farewell.

— *Regulations of the Lodge of Aberdeen*
(Scotland) of December 27, 1670

VII. Every New Brother at his making is decently to cloath the Lodge, that is all the Brethren present, and to deposite something for the Relief of indigent and decay'd Brethren, as the Candidate shall think fit to bestow, over and above the small Allowance stated by the By-Laws of that particular Lodge; which Charity shall be lodg'd with the Master or Wardens, or the Cashier, if the Members think fit to chuse one.

XIII. They shall also consider of the most prudent and effectual Methods of collecting and disposing of what Money shall be given to, or lodged with them in Charity, towards the Relief only of any true Brother fallen into Poverty or Decay, but none else: But every particular Lodge shall dispose of their own Charity for poor Brethren, according to their own By-Laws . . .

— General Regulations VII and XIII
Grand Lodge of England 1722

The Ancient Landmarks of Freemasonry, like all other landmarks, material or symbolical, can only preserve their stability, when they reach down to sure foundations. When the philosophic student unearths the underlying rock on which our Ancient Landmarks rest, he finds sure foundations in the triple dogma of the Fatherhood of God, the Brotherhood of Man, and the Life to come. All laws, customs, and methods that obtain amongst us and do not ultimately find footholds on this basis, are thereby earmarked as conventions and conveniences, no way partaking of the nature of Ancient Landmarks.

Many corallaries flow from these fundamental propositions: "and the greatest of these is Charity." What more logical or more obvious deducation can be conceived than the care of the Fatherless children of our Brethren?

— W. J. Chetwode Crawley
On Masonic Orphanages

You are cautiously to examine him, in such a Method as Prudence shall direct you, that you may not be impos'd upon by an ignorant false Pretender, whom you are to reject with Contempt and Derision, and beware of giving him any Hints of Knowledge.

But if you discover him to be a true and genuine Brother, you are to respect him accordingly; and if he is in want, you must relieve him if you can, or else direct him how he may be reliev'd: You must employ him some Days, or else recommend him to be employ'd. But you are not charged to go beyond your Ability, only to prefer a poor Brother, that is a good Man and true, before any other poor People in the same Circumstances.

— James Anderson
Old Charges from the Constitution of 1723

The term, "Masonic Benevolence," encompasses a wide spectrum of the acts of Brotherhood. It is a traditional example of "the Masonic Way." The first recorded act of Masonic Charity is found in the minutes of The Lodge of Edinburgh (Mary's Chapel) No. 1 of December 27, 1729.

> "And lastly The societie
> upon applicon from one
> David Mitchell/a poor dis-
> trest journayman mason
> appointed Henry Wilson/
> their former Warden to give
> him three pounds scots And
> to take/credite therefor in
> his accompts."

Since that time Masonic Lodges throughout the world have dispensed charity to poor and distressed Brethren and extended it to their widows and orphans. Charity contains the lubricant and the cement of life. It is an essential ingredient of Masonry. It has been said that "the Masonic Way is to give without remembering and to receive without forgetting."

— *The Short Talk Bulletin*
Vol. LVII, No. 11, November, 1979

Freemasonry has tenets peculiar to itself . . . The good effects they have produced are established by the most incontestable facts of history. They have stayed the uplifted hand of the destroyer; they have softened the asperities of the tyrant; they have mitigated the horrors of captivity; they have subdued the rancour of malevolence; they have broken down the barriers of political animosity and sectarian alienation. On the field of battle, in the solitudes of the uncultivated forest, or in the busy haunts of the crowded city, they have made men of the most hostile feelings, the most distant regions, and diversified conditions, rush to the aid of each other, and feel a special joy and satisfaction that they have been able to afford relief to a Brother Mason.

— Benjamin Franklin

. . . [Masonic charity] has proved so eminently successful in relieving every case brought to the attention of the Trustees, that it is given the most hearty and generous support by the Grand and Subordinate Lodges of Iowa. The hearts of the beneficiaries are made glad by the assistance that comes to them in the hour of need, not as a bounden duty faithfully performed, but rather as prompted by the spirit of brotherly love and relief, which are the principal tenets of our profession; for we are Masons not for what we may get, but for what we may attain, what we may do for others. *This is our glory;* this is what makes Masonry the synonym of charity throughout the civilized world; this is what will shine brighter luster upon her fair name, as the centuries one by one shall be added to the past, even down to 'the last syllable of time.'

— William F. Cleveland
History of the Grand Lodge of Iowa, Vol. Two

When our love or desire of good goes forth to others, it is term-ed good-will or benevolence. Benevolence embraces all beings capable of enjoying any portion of good; and thus it becomes universal benevolence, which manifests itself by being pleased with the share of good every creature enjoys, in a disposition to in-crease it, in feeling an uneasiness at their sufferings, and in the abhorrence of cruelty under every disguise or pretext. It is this spirit which should pervade the hearts of all Masons, who are taught to look upon mankind as formed by the Great Architect of the Universe for the mutual assistance, instruction, and support by each other.

—Albert G. Mackey
Encyclopedia of Freemasonry

The exclusiveness of Masonic benevolence is a charge that has frequently been made against the Order; it is said that the charity of which it boasts is always conferred on its own members in preference to strangers. It cannot be denied that Masons, simply as Masons, have ever been more constant and more profuse in their charities to their own brethren than to the rest of the world; that in apportioning the alms which God has given them to bestow, they have first looked for the poor in their own home before they sought those who were abroad; and that their hearts felt more deeply for the destitution of a Brother than a stranger.

The principle that governs the Institution of Freemasonry, in the distribution of its charities, and the exercise of all the friendly affections, is that laid down by St. Paul for the government of the infant church at Galatia: "As we have therefore opportunity, let us do good unto all men, especially unto them who are of the household of faith." (Galatians vi, 10.)

—Albert G. Mackey
Encyclopedia of Freemasonry

Although almsgiving, or the pecuniary relief of the destitute, was not one of the original objects for which the Institution of Freemasonry was established, yet, as in every society of men bound together by a common tie, it becomes incidentally, yet necessarily, a duty to be practiced by all its members in their individual as well as in their corporate capacity. In fact, this virue is intimately interwoven with the whole superstructure of the Institution and its practice is a necessary corollary from all its principles. "The true Mason," says Brother Albert Pike, "must be, and must have a right to be, content with himself; and he can be so only when he lives not for himself alone, but for others who need his assistance and have a claim upon his sympathy."

—Albert G. Mackey
Encyclopedia of Freemasonry

• Give, looking for nothing again, without consideration of future advantages; give to children, to old men, to the unthankful, and the dying, and to those who shall never see again; for else your alms or courtesy is not charity, but traffic and merchandise. And omit not to relieve the needs of your enemy and him who does you injury.

• What we have done for ourselves alone dies with us; what we have done for others and the world remains and is immortal.

—Albert Pike

" . . . the three greatest moral forces are FAITH, which is the only true WISDOM, and the very foundation of government; HOPE, which is STRENGTH, and insures SUCCESS; and CHARITY, which is BEAUTY, and alone makes animated, united effort possible. These forces are within the reach of all men; and an association of men, actuated by them, ought to exercise an immense power in the world. If Masonry does not, it is because she has ceased to possess them.

* * *

"Charity is the great channel," it has been well said, "through which God passed all His mercy upon mankind. For we receive absolution of our sins in proportion to our forgiving our brother. This is the rule of our hopes and the measure of our desire in this world; and on the day of death and judgment, the great sentence upon mankind shall be transacted according to our alms, which is the other part of charity. God himself is love; and every degree of charity that dwells in us is the participation of divine nature."

* * *

Q.   What is the seventh great Truth in Masonry?
A.   The immutable law of God requires that besides respecting the rights of others, and being merely just, we should do good, be charitable, and obey the dictates of the generous and noble sentiments of the soul. Charity is a law, because our conscience is not satisfied nor at ease if we have not relieved the suffering, the distressed, and the destitute . . . To be charitable is obligatory on us. We are the Almoners of God's bounties . . .

—Albert Pike
Morals and Dogma

50

The word used by the apostle is in the original Greek, *agape,* or love, a word denoting that kindly state of mind which renders a person full of good-will and affectionate regard towards others. Guided by the sentiments expressed in 1 Corinthians xiii, 1, 2, the true Mason will "suffer long and be kind." He will be slow to anger and easy to forgive. He will stay his falling brother by gentle admonition, and warn him with kindness of approaching danger. He will not open his ear to his slanders, and will close his lips against all reproach. His faults and his follies will be locked in his heart, and the prayer for mercy will ascend to Jehovah for his brother's sins. Nor will these sentiments of benevolence be confined to those who are bound to him by ties of kindred or worldly friendship alone; but, extending them throughout the globe, he will love and cherish all who sit beneath the broad canopy of our universal Lodge. For it is the boast of our Institution, that a Mason, destitute and worthy, may find in every clime a brother, and in every land a home.

York Rite Masonry is a beneficent and charitable institution and assists symbolic Masonry in carrying on its charitable activities. Whenever disaster strikes, York Rite Masonry does its bit; floods, fire, hunger, epidemic — as well as the care of the young and old — whatever it may be — York Rite Masonry will be present. "By their works ye shall know them."

— *History of Royal Arch Masonry*
(A paraphrase)

Charity is a shining virtue, adorns our nature, comports with the feelings of humanity, and is deeply characteristic of true benevolence of heart. Hence Masonry, as a charitable Institution, aside from all other considerations, is justly entitled to the approbation of mankind. Individuals, in their private capacity, are never expected promptly to meet all the exigencies of innocent sufferers. Hence, the union of individuals will afford the more sure means of effecting this important object.

If charity to the destitute is a duty, and a charitable society a blessing to the country, then the Masonic Institution *deserves* the patronage of every benevolent, humane, and charitable person, and the applause of mankind in general, as a useful and important Institution. It is a wise, a universal and a permanent establishment. Not circumscribed, as to charitable donations, by country, or confined to nation, sect, age or condition, it considers all mankind the children of one common parent, and brethren in one great family. It shields from danger, and on some degrees will even feed an enemy at the point of a sword, should his necessities absolutely require it. Such charity is God-like. It forgives an enemy, and renders good for evil. It covers a multiple of faults. Such benevolent charity disarms the heart of all enemity and, if universally exercised, would restore and perpetuate universal peace to the world. Hence the principles of Speculative Freemasonry, in every shape, when carried into practice, aim directly at the alleviation of human misery, the advancement of the peace, the harmony and happiness of society, and friendship and brotherly affections of all the inhabitants of the earth.

— *Salem Town*

The doctrines of Masonry are the most beautiful that it is possible to imagine. They breathe the simplicity of the earliest ages animated by the love of a martyred God. The word which the Puritans translated Charity, but which is really Love, is the keystone which supports the entire edifice of this mystic science. Love one another, teach one another, help one another. This is all our doctrine, all our science, all our law.

— *W. Winwood Reade*
The Veil of Isis

What though a man win wealth and the applause of fame, and have not Charity, it is nothing; what though he sway the world with his eloquence and miss the high prize of "self-knowledge, self-reverence and self-control," even if man erect an obelisk of gold above his grave it is a monument to failure. He only is wise who lives a simple, sincere, faithful life, building on the Square by the Plumb, toiling in the light of Eternity.

—*Joseph Fort Newton*

Charity is the ultimate fulfillment of its two co-partners, Faith and Hope. We should promote its warming influence throughout the world and lovingly espouse that sentiment uniting those "who might otherwise have remained at a perpetual distance."

"Where there is Charity and Love, there the God of Love abides."

— *N. S. W. Freemason*

Masonic charity is strong, kindly, beautiful and tender, and not a charity at all in the narrow sense of the word. Nay, it does not wait until a brother is in distress, but throws about him in his strength and prosperity the affectionate arm of friendship, without which life is cold and harsh. Friendship, fraternity, fellowship—this is the soul of Freemasonry, of which charity is but one gesture with a thousand meanings.

Freemasonry not only inculcates the principles of love and benevolence, it seeks to give them an actual and living presence in all the occupations and intercourse of life. It not only feels, it acts! It not only pities human suffering, it relieves it! Nowhere in the world can a Mason feel himself alone, friendless or forsaken. The invisible but helpful arms of our Order surround him, wherever he may be . . .

It is a common error to regard charity as that sentiment which prompts us to extend assistance to the unfortuante. Charity in a Masonic sense has a much broader meaning, and embraces affection and goodwill toward all mankind, but more especially our brethren in Freemasonry. It is this sentiment which prompts a Freemason to suffer long and be kind, to control his temper, forgive the erring, reach forth his hand to stay a falling brother, to warn him of his error and whisper in his ear that correction which his fault may demand, to close his ear to slander and his lips to reproach; in short, to do unto others as he would be done by.

Charity as applied to Freemasonry is different from the usual and accepted meaning. All true Masons meet upon the same level, regardless of wealth or station. In giving assistance we strive the too common error of considering charity only as that sentiment of commiseration which leads us to assist the poor and unfortunate with pecuniary donations. Its Masonic application is more noble and more extensive. We are taught not only to relieve a brother's material wants, the cry of hunger, etc., but to fellowship with him upon his own level, stripped of worldly titles and honors. When we thus appeal to him, giving spiritual advice, lifting him up morally and spiritually with no sense of humiliation to him, we set him free from his passion and wants. To such charity there is a reciprocity rich in brotherly love and sincere appreciation.

— Carl H. Claudy

We do not ordinarily think of Masonry as a mission nor of Masons as missionaries, but if we believe deeply what we espouse and would win the world to our way of living and believing, it must be done "out there" where the action is, where the people are!

Cloistered Masons (locked safely away from the rest of the world in their lodge rooms) may well go the way of the cloistered convents and monasteries of another era.

Masons having a calling to build within themselves better characters; and within their communities, a better society. Our Masonic missions include the total welfare of all mankind, the causes of constitutional government and true patriotism, and the support of the public schools and the education of the masses. Masons should accept their call to serve as masonic missionaries.

— *Woodrow W. Morris*
This I Believe

One of the foundations upon which Freemasonry stands is our deep and abiding concern for the needs of our fellow men, and a desire to be of service to mankind.

— *Woodrow W. Morris*

Too many members of our fraternity have failed to realize or have forgotten the great philosophical principle of charity which is an integral part of the fabric of our fraternity's teachings. Too often we think of charity in its monetary context which is the smallest facet of this great principle. To help, aid, assist, support, whisper good counsel, relieve the distressed, comfort, sympathize, and promote a brother's welfare, to remind a brother of his errors, not to speak unkindly to him, are all manifestations and a part of the teachings of Masonic Charity in its truest form.

To understand the true meaning of charity is only to understand the use of this working tool. A tool which is of no value unless it is applied by the workman for its designed purpose in the meaningful production for which it was intended. A rededication and reorientation of ourselves to this principle is essential if we, as Masons, are to serve each other and our fellow man . . .

If we fail to realize and practice the charity of our teachings, we also fail to realize that some day we, too, may be infirm or in need — then can we expect *that* which we ourselves may have failed to provide? No, my brethren, we have failed ourselves and have cheated ourselves from experiencing that wonderful personal feeling of well-being which accompanies and rewards acts of charity. We have failed our brethren and our fraternity by our inadequate attention to that supreme principle of Jacob's Ladder — CHARITY. THIS I BELIEVE.

— *Tom Corothers*
This I Believe

Masons in the early days of the guilds, before the Lodges were formed, recognized the importance of charity for the less fortunate, and on each Patron Saint's day they regularly provided funds for that purpose. For each Mason learns in the First Degree—"Charity extends beyond the grave, through the boundless ages of eternity."

Accordingly, we Masons recognize there must be a greater charity than that of giving of our substance. And there is. It is the gift that no one else but you can give. It is the giving of ourselves—the giving of time and talents in a thousand different ways to our churches and synagogues, our schools, our Lodges, hospitals, Little Leagues, Boy and Girl Scouts, DeMolays, Rainbow Girls, Job's Daughters and others. Through these acts we *personally* help the weak, the poor, the needy, the sick and those requiring our care and love.

Think for a moment of the giving of yourself by extending the charity of compassion to those with whom you may not agree. Or consider how Masons are the first to extend our hands in friendship to those who would despitefully use us . . . "The individual who would truly exemplify Brotherly Love comes closest to Heaven on Earth."

It is entirely conceivable that the guidance of the so-called Patron Saints of the medieval Masons indoctrinated a concern for others, a responsibility to the guild and subsequent Lodge members.

Thus down through the ages came the importance of the men of Masonry in the giving of charity or relief in its many forms including financial help and relief for the distressed in body, mind and spirit. How proud those early Masons would be to see the great philanthropic work of their counterparts today providing extensive humanitarian service to all mankind in the giving of themselves and their substance in a manner unparalleled in the history of all the world.

— Chester R. MacPhee
Masons: Knights of Charity
The New Age, November, 1981

Freemasonry, is it the same as yesteryear? Are our accomplishments as great? Is our work as meaningful? Are Masons as charitable as they once were?

There are many beautiful faces to Masonry: the child who walks through life instead of crawling; the child who goes to sleep minus the pangs of hunger; the child who wakes up to see that Santa did not pass him or her by; the child who at least for a moment escapes the ghetto and sees nature in full bloom; the young people who can further their education because scholarship money is available; the Masonic Widow who is given support to face life after her loss; the fallen Brother who ever so gently is lifted back to his feet; the Masonic Homes for the elderly where care and love abound.

*   *   *

You may recall reading an essay written by Washington Irving in which he stated that, "He who plants an oak looks forward to future ages, and plants for posterity. Nothing can be less selfish than this. He cannot expect to sit in its shade nor enjoy its shelter, but he exults in the idea that the acorn he has buried in the earth shall grow up into a lofty tree and shall keep flourishing and increasing and benefitting mankind long after he shall have ceased to tread this earth."

Our Masonic forefathers planted an acorn many centuries ago which has grown into a lofty monument and as the mighty oak provides a refuge for the weak, a shelter for the oppressed, a defense for the defenseless, as does our Fraternity provide Faith, Hope and Charity for our needy Brothers. Once again, we in Masonry have an opportunity to flourish in our communities by giving to our elderly citizens that life blood which has surged through our root system. *Faith* that there can be a bright tomorrow; *Hope* when the burdens of life seem to bear down too hard; and the *Charity* of Love.

— *Charles M. Menge*
Reach Out and Touch Someone
Short Talk Bulletin
The Masonic Service Association

In a Masonic sense, charity is defined in at least two parts of our rituals. In each, charity is synonymous with service, and service is synonymous with humanitarian love. The first explanation is given within the meaning of our Great Guiding Lights. We are instructed that the Holy Bible is dedicated to the service of Deity. Since, I believe, the words service, charity, and humanitarian love are interchangeable, this phrase could be restated as the Holy Bible is dedicated to charitable actions which are done in the name of God and for humanity.

A second explanation is given in the First Degree, where we are told that Jacob constructed a ladder which extended from earth to heaven. The principle rungs . . . were denoted as Faith, Hope, and Charity. It also implied that of these three "living truths," Faith and Hope are the most tentative . . . Charity, however, survives the grave and provides a legacy of notable benchmarks by which man's life can be measured and valued.

* * *

. . . Masonic charity is clearly a matter of heart and hand, belief and practice, in all areas of fraternal life. It extends from within the character and development of the individual Brother to his Lodge Brethren, to the Craft's many philanthropies, to the community at large. Focused and built on the single Mason, it moves to all mankind. They say "charity begins at home." True, but the "home" of Freemasonry reaches beyond its tiled doors to the entire world and all its peoples. We are all children of God and His universal law, and as the immortal bard Shakespeare said:

"Charity itself fulfills the law,
And who can sever love from charity?"

— *Henry C. Doster*
Masonic Charity
The New Age, February, 1983

Ann Layman Chancellor

To the glory of God and for all in need
  regardless of race, color, or creed;
Never does a Shriner stand so tall
  as when he stoops to break the fall
Of a child who is crippled, hurt, or burned
  for those are our hospitals' deep concern.
And we know, with our trust in the Heavenly throne—
  neither child nor Shriner will ever walk alone.

> *—A song composed by*
> *E. H. "Bus" Gulick for the*
> *Abu Bekr Shrine Chanters*

Strong legs run so weak legs may walk.

No man stands so tall as when he stoops to help a crippled child.

Help a Shriner help a child.

Shriners Burn Unit credo:

  Care
  Research
  Teaching
  Prevention

> We can't put a price on what we do
> for kids, so we do it for free . . .
> Today's research is tomorrow's patient care.
> Shriners Hospitals daily give children
> a reason to smile.
>
> *—Slogans used by the Shrine in*
> *promoting their Hospitals for*
> *Crippled Children and Burn Units*

CHARITY — A NEW MEANING

The "box of fraternal assistance" which once occupied the central position in every Masonic lodge room has been replaced by an annual per capita tax. That benevolence which for ages has been one of the sweetest by-products of the teachings of our gentle craft has, I fear, ceased to be a gift from the heart and has become the writing of a check. And unless the personal element is there, charity becomes as sounding brass and a tinkling cymbal.

Given the challenge to practice Masonic charity in its intimate and personal form, almost any lodge and almost any individual Mason will respond with enthusiasm. More important, Freemasonry will then come to have a new meaning for them.

— Dwight L. Smith
Whither Are We Traveling
The Indiana Freemason

ACCORDING TO STATESMEN

Ann Layman Chancellor

You cannot be buried in obscurity:
    You are exposed upon a grand theater to the view of the world.
        If your actions are upright and benevolent,
            be assured they will augment your power and happiness.
                                — *Cyrus the Great*

For forms of government let fools contest;
Whate'er is best adminster'd is best:
For modes of faith let graceless zealots fight;
His can't be wrong whose life is in the right.
In faith and hope the world will disagree,
But all mankind's concern is charity.
                  — *Alexander Pope*
                  An Essay on Man, Epistle II

That religion, or duty which we owe
to our Creator, and the manner of
discharging it, can be directed only
by reason and conviction, not by
force or violence; and therefore all
men are equally entitled to the free
exercise of religion, according to the
dictates of conscience; and that is
the mutual duty of all to practice
Christian forbearance, love, and
charity towards each other.
          — *Patrick Henry*
          Virginia Bill of Rights

Be rather bountiful than expensive;
    do good with what thou hast,
        or it will do thee no good.
              — *William Penn*

Real goodness does not attatch itself merely to this life — it points to another world. Political or professional reputation cannot last forever, but a conscience void of offence before God and man is an inheritance for eternity.

— Daniel Webster

Government is a contrivance of human wisdom to provide for human wants. Men have a right that these wants should be provided by this wisdom.

— Edmund Burke

In charity to all mankind, bearing no malice or ill-will to any human being, or even compassionating those who hold in bondage their fellow men, not knowing what they do.

— John Quincy Adams

I deem it the duty of every man to devote a certain portion of his income for charitable purposes; and that it is his further duty to see it so applied and to do the most good of which it is capable. This I believe to be best insured by keeping within the circle of his own inquiry and information the subjects of distress to whose relief his contributions should be applied.

— *Thomas Jefferson*
Writings, Vol. XI

I believe that every human mind feels pleasure in doing good for another.

— *Thomas Jefferson*
Letter to John Adams

The principle of liberty and equality, if coupled with mere selfishness, will make men only devils, each trying to be independent that he may fight only for his own interest. And here is the need of religion and its power, to bring the principle of benevolence and love to men.

—*John Randolph*

With malice toward none; with charity for all; with firmness in the right, as God gives us to see the right, let us strive to finish the work we are in; to bind up the nation's wounds; to care for him who shall have borne the battle and for his widow, and his orphan — to do all which may achieve and cherish a just and lasting peace among ourselves, and with all nations.

— Abraham Lincoln
Second Inaugural Address

A really great man is known by three signs —
generosity in the design,
humanity in the execution,
moderation in success.

— Otto Eduard Bismarck

The proper function of government is to make it easy for people to do good and difficult for them to do evil.

— William E. Gladstone

I feel obliged to withhold my approval of the plan to indulge a benevolent and charitable sentiment through the appropriation of public funds for that purpose (i.e., to distribute seeds to drought-stricken counties of Texas in 1887). I can find no warrant for such an appropriation in the Constitution.

— Grover Cleveland

A man who is good enough to shed his blood for his country is good enough to be given a square deal afterwards. More than that no man is entitled to, and less than that no man shall have.

— Theodore Roosevelt

My country owes me nothing. It gave me, as it gives every boy and girl, a chance. It gave me schooling, independence of action, opportunity for sevice and honor. In no other land could a boy from a country village, without inheritance or influential friends, look forward with unbounded hope.

— *Herbert Hoover*

No person was ever honored for what he received. Honor has been the reward for what he gave.

— *Calvin Coolidge*

The nature of men of organized society dictates the maintenance in every field of action of the highest and purest standards of justice and of right dealing . . . By justice the lawyer generally means the prompt, fair, and open application of impartial laws; but we call ours a Christian civilization, and a Christian conception of justice must be higher. It must include sympathy and helpfulness and a willingness to forego self-interest in order to promote the welfare, happiness, and contentment of others and of the community as a whole.

— *Woodrow Wilson*

I see one-third of a nation ill-housed, ill-clad, ill-nourished. The test of our progress is not whether we add more to the abundance of those who have much; it is whether we provide enough for those who have too little.

— *Franklin Delano Roosevelt*

Government can err. Presidents do make mistakes, but the immortal Dante tells us that divine justice weighs the sins of the cold-blooded and the sins of the warm-hearted in different scales. Better the occasional faults of a government that lives in a spirit of charity than the consistent omissions of a government frozen in the ice of its own indifference.

— *Franklin Delano Roosevelt*

. . . as new conditions and problems arise beyond the power of men and women to meet as individuals, it becomes the duty of Government itself to find new remedies with which to meet them . . . the Government has the definite duty to use all its powers and resources to meet new social problems with new social controls — to insure to the average person the right to his own economic and political life, liberty, and the pursuit of happiness.

— *Franklin Delano Roosevelt*

We must embark on a bold new program for making the benefits of our scientific advances and industrial progress available for the improvement and growth of underdeveloped areas. More than half of the people of the world are living in conditions approaching misery. Their food is inadequate. They are the victims of disease. Their economic life is primitive and stagnant. Their poverty is a handicap and a threat both to them and to more prosperous areas.

— Harry S. Truman
Inaugural Address, 1949

I rather think there is an immense shortage of Christian charity among so-caled Christians.

— Harry S. Truman

A hungry man is not a free man.
— Adlai Stevenson

You can't run a government solely on a business basis . . . Government should be human. It should have a heart.

— Herbert Lehman

Humanitarianism is a link that binds together all Americans . . . Whenever tragedy or disaster has struck in any corner of the world, the American people have promptly and generously extended its hand of mercy and help. Generosity has never impoverished the giver; it has enriched the lives of those who have practiced it . . . And the bread we have cast upon the waters has been returned in blessings a hundredfold.

— Dwight D. Eisenhower

Ann Layman Chancellor

When we say a patriot is one who loves his country, what kind of love do we mean? A love we can throw on a scale and see how much it weighs? A love we can take apart to see how it ticks? A love where with a yardstick we record how long, high, wide, it is? Or is a patriot's love of country a thing invisible, a quality, a human shade and breath, beyond all reckoning and measurement? These are questions. They are as old as the time of man. And the answers to them we know in part. For we know when a nation goes down and never comes back, when a society or a civilization perishes, one condition may always be found. They forgot where they came from. They lost sight of what brought them along. The hard beginnings were forgotten and the struggles farther along. They became satisfied with themselves. Unity and common understanding there had been, enough to overcome rot and dissolution, enough to break through their obstacles. But the mockers came. And the deniers were heard. And vision and hope faded. And the custom of greeting became "What's the use?" And men whose forefathers would go anywhere, holding nothing impossible in the genius of man, joined the mockers and deniers. They forgot where they came from. They lost sight of what had brought them along.

When we say a patriot is one who loves his country, what kind of love is it we mean? These are tremendous questions. I could write a book trying to answer those questions. You have heard that the shroud has no pockets and the dead to whatever place they go carry nothing with them — you have heard that and you know its meaning is plain. Whatever cash or collateral a man may have had, whatever bonds, securities, deeds and titles to land, real estate, buildings, leases and patents, whatever of jewels, medals, decorations, keepsakes or costly apparel, he leaves them all behind and goes out of the world naked and bare as he came. You have also heard the dead hold in their clenched hands only that which they have given away. In this we begin to approach the meaning of a patriot though we do not unlock the secret that hides in the bosom of a patriot. The dead hold in their clenched hands only that which they have given away. When men forget what is at the heart of that sentiment—and it is terribly sentimental—they are in danger of power being taken over by swine, or beasts of prey or men hollow with echoes and vanities. It has happened and the records and annals cry and moan with specific instances.

*   *   *

In a very real sense there is no such thing as a death of thought and energy. The will and vision that motivated people in Plymouth did not fade but moved on alive and written on faces at Valley Forge. It is still with us. Generations vanish, people disappear, the earth stays and the transmission of energy. Life goes on.

Long before this time of ours America saw the faces of her men and women torn and shaken in turmoil, chaos, and storm. In each major crisis you could have seen despair written on the faces of the foremost strugglers. Yet there always arose enough of reserves of strength, balances of sanity, portions of wisdom, to carry the nation through to a fresh start with an ever renewing vitality.

You may bury the bones of men and later dig them up to find they have moldered into a thin white ash that crumbles in your fingers. But their ideas won. Their visions came through. Men and women who gave all they had and wished they had more to give—how can we say they are sunk and buried? They live in the sense that their dream is on the faces of living men and women today. In a rather real sense the pioneers, old settlers, First Comers as some called themselves—they go on, their faces here now, their lessons worth our seeing. They ought not to be forgotten—the dead who held in their clenched hands that which became the heritage of us, the living.

— *Carl Sandburg*
Remembrance Rock

ACCORDING TO MANKIND

The charities of life are scatterd everywhere,
    enameling the vales of human beings
    as the flowers paint the meadows.
They are not the fruit of study,
    nor the privilege of refinement,
    but the natural instinct.

— George Bancroft

Generosity during life is a very different thing from generosity in the hour of death; one proceeds from genuine liberality and benevolence, the other from pride or fear.

— Horace Mann

A man there was, they called him mad;
the more he gave, the more he had.

—John Bunyan

The heart has reasons that reason does not understand.

—Jacques Benigne Bossuet

To feel much for others,
    and little for ourselves;
    to restrain our selfish and
    exercise our benevolent affections,
    constitutes the perfection of
    human nature.

— Adam Smith

Man is honored for his wisdom, loved for his kindness.

— Shalom Cohen

There never was a man who did anything worth doing who did not receive more than he gave.

— Henry Ward Beecher

The best thing to give to your enemy is forgiveness;
  to an opponent, tolerance;
  to a friend, your heart;
  to your child, a good example;
  to a father, deference;
  to your mother, conduct that will make her proud of you;
  to yourself, respect;
  to all men, charity.

— Francis Maitland Balfour

Put yourself in the other fellow's place,
and you will have freed your soul from the
spirit of caste.

— Stephen S. Wise

Charity is the sterilized milk of human kindness.

— Oliver Herford

If a body's ever took charity, it
makes a burn that don't come out.

— John Steinbeck

The happiness of love is in action;
Its test is what one is willing to do for others.

— Lew Wallace

Compassion is the chief law of human existence.

— Fyodor M. Dostoievski

I believe in the supreme worth of the individual and in his right to
    life, liberty, and the pursuit of happiness.

I believe that every right implies a responsibility; every
    opportunity, an obligation; every possession, a duty.

I believe that the law was made for man and not man for the law; that
    government is the servant of the people and not their master.

I believe in the dignity of labor, whether with head or hand; that
    the world owes no man a living but that it owes every man an
    opportunity to make a living.

I believe that thrift is essential to well ordered living and that
    economy is a prime requisite of a sound financial structure,
    whether in government, business, or personal affairs.

I believe that truth and justice are fundamental to an enduring
    social order.

I believe in the sacredness of a promise, that a man's word should
    be as good as his bond; that character — not wealth or power
    or position — is of supreme worth.

I believe that the rendering of useful service is the common duty
    of mankind and that only in the purifying fire of sacrifice is
    the dross of selfishness consumed and the greatness of the
    human soul set free.

I believe in an all-wise and all-loving God, named by whatever
    name, and that the individual's highest fulfillment, greatest
    happiness, and widest usefulness are to be found in living in
    harmony with His will.

I believe that love is the greatest thing in the world; that it alone can
    overcome hate; that right can and will triumph over might.

John D. Rockefeller, Jr.

A man has made at least a start on discovering the meaning of human life when he plants shade trees under which he knows full well he will never sit.

— *Elton Trueblood*

A man is as great as the dreams he dreams,
As great as the love he bears,
As great as the values he redeems,
And the happiness he shares.
     A man is as great as the thoughts he thinks,
     As the worth he has attained,
     As the fountains at which his spirit drinks,
     As the insight he has gained.
          A man is as great as the truths he speaks,
          As great as the help he gives,
          As great as the destiny he seeks,
          As great as the life he lives.

— *Anonymous*

Love never looks for faults, and whenever it discovers them in others it throws over them the mantle of charity and performs the twofold miracle of making itself more beautiful and the one in whom the fault is found more happy.

— *Edward Emmett*

Money giving is a very good criterion, in a way, of a person's mental health. Generous people are rarely mentally ill people.

— *Karl Menninger*

Ann Layman Chancellor

BROTHERHOOD

Each of us
is different from the other.
One man's weakness
may be your strength
while his strength
may be your weakness.
Thus
we need one another.
The lonely need friendship
the sick need care
the feeble need support
the frightened, comfort
for man has many weaknesses
and many strengths.

It is this constant giving
of one's self
and receiving from others
that brings happiness,
nothing more.

Just as the pitcher which is emptied
and refilled
many times a day
remains sparkling
and gives the sweetest water.

Give then each day
a little of your time
your friendship
your sympathy
your understanding
even of your physical assistance
and what you get in return
will brighten your life
a thousand ways:

And when you have done
all these things
you will have discovered
the true meaning
of Brotherhood.

    — Martin Buxbaum
     The Underside of Heaven

Strange is our situation here on earth. Each of us comes for a short visit, not knowing why, yet sometimes seeming to divine a purpose.

From the standpoint of daily life, however, there is one thing we do know: that man is here for the sake of other men—above all for those upon whose smile and well-being our own happiness depends, and also for the countless unknown souls with whose fate we are connected by a bond of sympathy. Many times a day I realize how much my own outer and inner life is built upon the labors of my fellow-men, both living and dead, and how earnestly I must exert myself in order to give in return as much as I have received. My peace of mind is often troubled by the depressing sense that I have borrowed too heavily from the work of other men.

—Albert Einstein

If everyone were perfect . . . in his
body, soul and mind . . . then the folks
who had compassion . . . would be
mighty hard to find . . . For each living
thing that suffers . . . is a challenge to
the rest . . . It's God's own way of
measuring . . . the kindness in your
breast.

it was intended to be
we loving them
and God loving us
faults and all.

— *Martin Buxbaum*
Rivers of Thought

The world has many happy folks . . .
who smile each day they live . . .
because they know that happiness . . .
depends on what you give.

For a giving man is different . . .
from his neighbors in the pod . . .
when his thoughts are of his brothers . . .
then he's closest to his God.

And the spark of love he kindles . . .
in a breast where hope has died . . .
sheds a warmth that's like no other . . .
for it feels so good inside.

And every time he gives a bit . . .
he adds a little part . . .
to that something deep within him . . .
that the poets call — a heart.

— Martin Buxbaum

By what standards do we measure a culture? It is customary to evaluate a nation by the magnitude of its scientific contributions or the quality of its artistic achievements. However, the true standard by which we gauge a culture is the extent to which reverence, compassion, justice are to be found in the daily lives of a whole people, not only in the acts of isolated individuals. Culture is a style of living compatible with the grandeur of being human.

—Abraham J. Heschel
To Grow in Wisdom
White House Conference on Aging, 1961

Proverbs from Many Lands and Peoples

Chinese:
- In accommodating others you accomodate yourself.
- Thinking of others' advantage will turn out to be one's own.
- Bowing in the dark is according to every man's fancy. (i.e., to do good secretly is optional.)
- If you are charitable you cannot become rich; if you are rich you cannot be charitable.
- The door to charity is hard to open and hard to shut.
- Deal with the faults of others as gently as with your own.
- Be forgetful of favours given; be mindful of blessings received.
- In good works do not yield place to others.

Dutch:
- When one friend washes another, both become clean.

Egyptian:
- Conceal the good you do, take example from the Nile which hides its source.

English:
- Charity bread has hard crusts.
- The comforter's head never aches.
- Do good, thou dost it for thyself.

89

Estonian:
- Where you find fault come and help.
- Forgive others everything, yourself nothing.
- He who helps the poor lends to God.
- A good deed bears less interest.
- The tip of the nose is to be seen, but not the end of kindness.

Finnish:
- No one is too poor to help another and no one is too rich to need help.

French:
- It is giving nothing not to give oneself.
- When doing good we never know all the good that we do.
- To fold hands (i.e., to pray) is well; to open them (i.e., to give) is better.

German:
- Charity gives itself riches; covetousness hoards itself poor.
- Charity looks at the need and not at the cause.
- Charity is a stately plant; its very rare flower is gratitude.

Greek:
- Unfading are the gardens of kindness.

Hebrew:
- Charity, that which is given in health, is gold; in sickness, silver; after death, lead.

Hindu:
- The raft of the benevolent gets across.

Hindustani:
- Charity protects you.
- Charity is a plant whose roots are evergreen.
- What thou givest shall be thy shield.
- What the hand has given will be a bar to misfortune.
- Philanthropy is true religion.

Hungarian:	• Did you give, forget it; did you accept, mention it.
	• If you give, give easily; if you accept, accept cheerily.
	• Not he who has, but he who wants to.
Indian:	• Do good and cast it upon the waters.
	• Be it a grain of pea-seed, let it be given with love.
Irish:	• No good is got by waste, but a good name is got by alms giving.
	• A good deed boasted of is little; a good deed not acknowledged is little better.
	• Water for the goose and alms for the beggar.
	• A generous man, they say, has never gone to hell.
	• Live in my heart and pay no rent.
	• The biggest help is help, and even the smallest help is help.
Italian:	• It is easier to comfort than to be comforted.
	• A kind action should close the mouth of him who does it, and open the mouth of him who receives it.
	• Love, alms, devotion, and patience are the four elements which make a man a saint.
	• Succour never comes too late.
Jamaican:	• The best passion is compassion.
	• "Do little" better than "point finger." (i.e., Little help better than criticism.)
	• Put me down softly, me a cracked plate.
Japanese:	• If you want to get on in the world, first help others to get on.
	• One good deed is better than three days of fasting at a shrine.
	• One good word can warm three winter months.
	• He has a big hand (i.e., liberal) (Korean)
	• There is no sword against kindness.

91

Latin:	• In things necessary, unity; in things doubtful, liberty; in all things, charity.
	• Not your good word, but your charity.
	• You still possess what you have given.
	• He gives twice who gives promptly.
	• Give the right hand to the wretched.
Moorish:	• If you have much give from your wealth, and if you have little give from your heart.
	• In everything offered there is good.
	• Good for good, and he who begins is more generous.
	• Do good and you will find good.
Persian:	• Help thou thy brother's boat across and lo, thine own has touched the shore.
	• Take the cotton out of thine ear and distribute justice to mankind.
	• He who gives little gives from his heart, but he who gives much gives from his fortune.
	• He needs no other rosary whose thread of life is strung with the beads of love and thought.
Polish:	• Forgive others easily but yourself never.
Portuguese:	• Give a grateful man more than he asks.
Russian:	• It is not the gift which is precious, it is the love.
	• A kind word is like a Spring day.
Sanskrit:	• He who allows his days to pass without practicing generosity and enjoying life's pleasure is like the blacksmith's bellows—he breaches but lives not.

Scottish:	• Charity ne'er made a man poor, nor robbing rich nor prosperity wise. • Giving to the poor increaseth a man's store. • Spend, and God will send; spare, and be bare. • Kindness comes of will, it cannot be bought. • He doubles his gift who gies't in time. • There are aye gude that gies. • Give your heart to God, and your alms to the poor. • It's a feeble hand that can't do good when the heart is willing. • Charity should begin at home but shouldna end there.
Spanish:	• The good that is done today constitutes the happiness of tomorrow.
Swedish:	• The light shines for others—not for itself.
Turkish:	• He who gives to the poor lends to God.
Unknown:	• There is so much good in the worst of us, And so much bad in the best of us, That it ill behoves any of us, To find fault with the rest of us. • The best gifts are tied with heart strings.
Welsh:	• There is a measure for everything, but there is no measure for charity. • The hand that gives, gathers.

AUTHOR INDEX & SUBJECT INDEX

Ann Layman Chancellor

INDEX OF AUTHORS

SUBJECT INDEX

106

111